PITTSBURGH
PENNSYLVANIA

A PHOTOGRAPHIC PORTRAIT

PHOTOGRAPHY BY MARK BOLSTER

First published in the United States of
America by:

Twin Lights Publishers, Inc.
8 Hale Street
Rockport, Massachusetts 01966
Telephone: (978) 546-7398
http://www.twinlightspub.com

ISBN: 1-885435-76-2
ISBN: 978-1-885435-76-7

10 9 8 7 6 5 4 3 2 1

Alcoa Corporate Center *(opposite)*

Completed in 1998, Alcoa's elegant,
"green built" corporate headquarters
unfurls along the North Shore and the
Allegheny River. Built with 800,000
pounds of Alcoa aluminum and 70,000
square feet of exterior glass, its wave-
form façade opens the entire building
to the river and city.

(jacket front)

The steel skyscrapers of Pittsburgh's
"Golden Triangle" business center illumi-
nate the night sky, while over the Monongahela River, Fort Pitt Bridge connects
the city's South Side with historic Point
State Park.

(jacket back)

Point State Park, on the site of historic
Fort Pitt, is a popular venue for many of
Pittsburgh's festivals and celebrations.
The three rectangular buildings are recre-
ations of three of Fort Pitt's original five
bastions, one of which is the Fort Pitt
Museum.

Editorial researched and written by:
Francesca and Duncan Yates
www.freelancewriters.com

Book design by:
SYP Design & Production, Inc.
www.sypdesign.com

Printed in China

The birthplace of America's steel industry in the 19th century, the city of Pittsburgh has experienced one of the most dramatic transformations and resurgences in the history of the United States. Pittsburgh is renowned as a center for academic pursuits and rich cultural venues. From its humble beginnings as a one-industry town, the "City of Bridges" has grown into a vibrant center of international business with a metro area population of over two million residents and a strong core of technological and financial institutions.

Pittsburgh's stoic journey from a once vital steel and iron manufacturing and mining town to a world-class center of modern enterprise has earned high praise. *USA Weekend Magazine* called Pittsburgh's panoramic vista "the second most beautiful view in America." In 2007, it was ranked America's most livable city for the second time by *Places Rated Almanac*.

Pittsburgh's quick rise to influence during the 18th and 19th centuries was due to the perfect combination of geography and geology. The city was settled on a strategically significant location where the Allegheny and Monongahela Rivers meet to form the Ohio River. Fort Pitt, a major British fortification during colonial times, would later grow to become the town of Pittsburgh. The hills surrounding the river valley, rich with coal deposits, kept America warm in the winter, and fired the furnaces of the burgeoning steel industry.

Pittsburgh has also profited immensely from the unprecedented philanthropy of its steel tycoons whose legacy is evident throughout the city. Multi-million-dollar endowments from Andrew Carnegie, Henry Clay Frick, and Andrew W. Mellon have built many of Pittsburgh's world-class museums, libraries, and educational institutions.

The dynamic Pittsburgh Cultural District spans fourteen blocks in the heart of downtown with five internationally-acclaimed performance halls, theaters, art-filled green spaces, dozens of restaurants, and nearly one-hundred shops and boutiques. This major tourist attraction pulses with energy and unbridled creativity.

With so many outstanding examples of bridge and tunnel design, Pittsburgh has earned the title "City of Bridges." Thirty major trestles and hundreds of bridges cross the city's rivers linking neighborhoods, while there are over 2,000 bridges in Allegheny County. Bridge architects and builders regularly hold their conventions here.

Pittsburgh is an eclectic patchwork of ethnic neighborhoods that envelop the gentle hills and steep slopes of the city's rocky terrain. Their residents include the descendants of 19th- and 20th-century immigrants from Europe and Russia, as well as freed slaves who found work in the region's steel mills and coal mines.

Resident commercial photographer Mark Bolster captures the renaissance of this great American city. With his compelling use of graphic composition and moody light, Bolster presents inspiring images in this dramatic photographic portrait.

City of Bridges (*opposite*)

A cable car makes its vertical ascent along the Monongahela Incline rising 635 feet to the the South Side neighborhood. Far below, skyscrapers sparkle in the "Golden Triangle" business district, while an array of bridges span massive rivers.

West End Overlook

Pittsburgh nestles in the triangular point of land where the Monongahela River from the southeast and the Allegheny River from the northeast meet to form the Ohio River. With this pivotal location, Pittsburgh has become one of the largest inland ports in the United States. It is a city with a hilly terrain where some neighborhoods, predominantly on the South Side, are quite steep. Thirty bridges cross the rivers and connect the city with the greater metropolitan area, home to over two million residents.

View from the North Shore

The decline of the steel industry resulted in a renaissance experience that included the most massive environmental restoration in American history. Steel mills and forgeries were replaced with riverfront parks, a gleaming skyline, and thriving corporations.

Bridge of Sighs *(top)*

This impressive pedestrian bridge was named from the mournful sighs of newly convicted inmates as they crossed from the Allegheny County Courthouse to the old county jail, now the Family Court Building, to begin their prison term.

Macy's Clock *(bottom)*

Kaufmann's Department Store would eventually become Macy's, yet the famous clock at Smithfield Street and Fifth Avenue would remain. The beloved downtown icon, with its ornate design, is a popular landmark and meeting place.

One Mellon Center *(opposite)*

Pittsburgh's second tallest skyscraper touches the sky, rising fifty-four stories high. Headquarters of Mellon Financial Corporation, a Fortune 500 giant, the complex houses restaurants, banks, shops, and a light rail station at the plaza level.

Rachel Carson Bridge (*opposite*)

A rowing team glides past the massive foundations of the Rachel Carson Bridge, formerly the Ninth Street Bridge. One of several bridges on the Allegheny River, it is a tribute to pioneering environmentalist Rachel Carson, author of *Silent Spring*.

Allegheny River Bridges (*above*)

A lone boat motors along the Allegheny River. Recognized as the "City of Bridges," Pittsburgh is a popular location for bridge engineer conventions. The number and variety of bridges in form and design is unparalleled in the United States.

The Machine that Built Pittsburgh *(top)*

Station Square showcases the miraculous Bessemer converter. Invented by Sir Henry Bessemer, this unique blend of forced-air technology produced the world's first viable commercial steel which paved the way for the modern skyscraper.

Historic Smithfield Street Bridge *(bottom)*

With more than 1,700 bridges in Allegheny County, the Smithfield Street Bridge has the distinction of being the oldest one in the county. Listed on the National Register of Historic Places, this 1883 bridge crosses the Monongahela River.

Riverboat School

Every July, the Carnegie Science Center sends children to River Exploration Camp aboard the *Pittsburgh Voyager*. The camp highlights the wide varity of fish and birds along Pittsburgh's rivers as well as the waterways' delicate ecological balance.

A Gleaming Landmark *(above)*

A landmark of Pittsburgh's "Golden Triangle" business district, One Mellon Center shimmers in the setting sun. The corporate headquarters for Mellon Financial Corporation, the 54-story building is the second tallest in the city.

Crossing the Monongahela River *(opposite)*

Of Pittsburgh's many bridges, the Fort Pitt Bridge is considered to be the most beautiful entrance into the city, leading to scenic Point State Park. In the background, the silver spires of PPG Place, built between 1981 and 1984, sparkle in a clear, blue sky.

Indigo Rising *(above)*

Two of Pittsburgh's most recognizable skyscrapers, Oxford Centre and the U.S. Steel Tower, are awash in blue light as the sun drops below the horizon. Dusk plays clever tricks with fleeting light, creating subtle yet dramtic scenery.

Reflections *(opposite)*

The rippling reflection of the nearby Highmark Building in the steel and glass façade of the PPG Center creates the illusion of ornately-carved ivory in a sea of cool, blue silk.

Fort Pitt Bridge (top)

A tug boat pushes a barge along the Monongahela River and passes under Fort Pitt Bridge. Because of the dramatic vistas seen from this bridge, the *New York Times* named Pittsburgh "the only city in America with an entrance."

16th Street Bridge (bottom)

One of the historic Allegheny River bridges, the 16th Street Bridge, opened in 1923, replacing the city's last wooden, covered bridge. It connects the Strip District to the Northside and is embellished with bronze sea horse sculptures and armillary spheres.

Fountain of Rainbows

A rainbow within the cascading waters of the Point State Park fountain adds to the spectacle of Pittsburgh's official Fourth-of-July celebration, the Three Rivers Regatta. The largest inland regatta in the country, it regularly attracts over 400,000 people for a weekend of extreme water sports, shows, and races that culminate in a dazzling fireworks display over the water. The spectacular setting is where the Allegheny River and the Monongahela River meet to form the mighty Ohio River.

Herr's Island, Washington Landing

This intimate community of forty-two acres was once a former rendering plant, landfill, scrap yard, and meat-packing plant. When the owner finally sold the land, Pittsburgh developers reshaped this stretch of water-front into an attractive, luxury community.

Under the Shell

A team of rowers steady their shell. The Three Rivers Rowing Association sponsors rowing classes and events on the western bank of the Allegheny River on an island known as Washington's Landing.

Vietnam Veterans Memorial *(opposite)*

This evocative memorial is located between Heinz Field and the PNC Stadium, on the Allegheny River's north shore. The unique composition incorporates life-size statues of soldiers standing under a lotus leaf symbolizing the human spirit or soul.

Urban Waterfall *(above)*

Refreshing and rambling, water cascades artfully down the broad, flat stones in front of the headquarters of Equitable Resources Inc., a Pittsburgh-based natural gas company.

Allegheny River Bridges at Sunrise *(top)*

The stark, ridged lines of bridges that span across the Allegheny River are a sharp contrast to the soft pastel sky of their backdrop. A gorgeous sunrise drenches the city in a blush of purple, pink, and gold across the sky and is reflected in deep, still waters.

Dinner with a View *(bottom)*

A romantic window table at the Le Mont Restaurant, located atop Pittsburgh's venerable Mount Washington, offers up one of the most spectacular views in America.

PPG Center *(opposite)*

The glass spires of PPG Center bask in the glow of the setting sun. The six-building complex and plaza covers three city blocks in the heart of downtown Pittsburgh. The project was designed by acclaimed architects Philip Johnson and John Burgee.

Holidays at the Plaza *(opposite)*

The holiday season in Pittsburgh begins with the official tree lighting in the center of the ice skating rink at PPG Center Plaza. The six buildings of PPG Center encircle the central court, creating an intimate town-square feel.

Sparkle Season Fireworks *(above)*

Santa has a superb riverfront view of Point State Park's fireworks display during "Light Up Night." It's the official entry into "Sparkle Season," six weeks of non-stop festivities and celebrations that end with the New-Year's-Eve "First Night" bash.

Rachel Carson Bridge *(pages 28–29)*

From the shoreline of the Northside, the Rachel Carson Bridge stretches across the Allegheny River. Named for the pioneering ecologist and writer, the bridge is a symbol of Pittsburgh's 21st-century commitment to the environment.

Monongahela River Tours *(above)*

Gateway Clipper sightseeing boats dock on the Monongahela River after a sunset cruise. The company introduced river cruises in 1958 and continue to provide spectacular views of the riverfront city.

Twilight's "Golden Triangle"

Downtown Pittsburgh's "Golden Triangle" business district is ablaze with light as dusk darkens the evening sky. The city's famous renaissance in recent decades has reshaped the face of Pittsburgh with major renewal projects such as Point State Park, the Civic Arena, and Gateway Center. Behind the downtown skyline, the hills of the Northside rise up from the banks of the Allegheny River.

Historic Byham Theater *(above)*

Originally one of the country's foremost stage and vaudeville theaters, the 1901 performance hall now showcases its former grandeur after extensive renovations inside and out. Today, it is a popular venue for live theater, opera, dance, and big-name shows.

Night Lights *(opposite)*

Rising 45 stories above the "Golden Triangle," One Oxford Centre is one of Pittsburgh's most distinctive skyscrapers. Ablaze with the illumination of forty-three mega-watt spotlights, it is recognized as the most brilliantly lit high-rise in the United States.

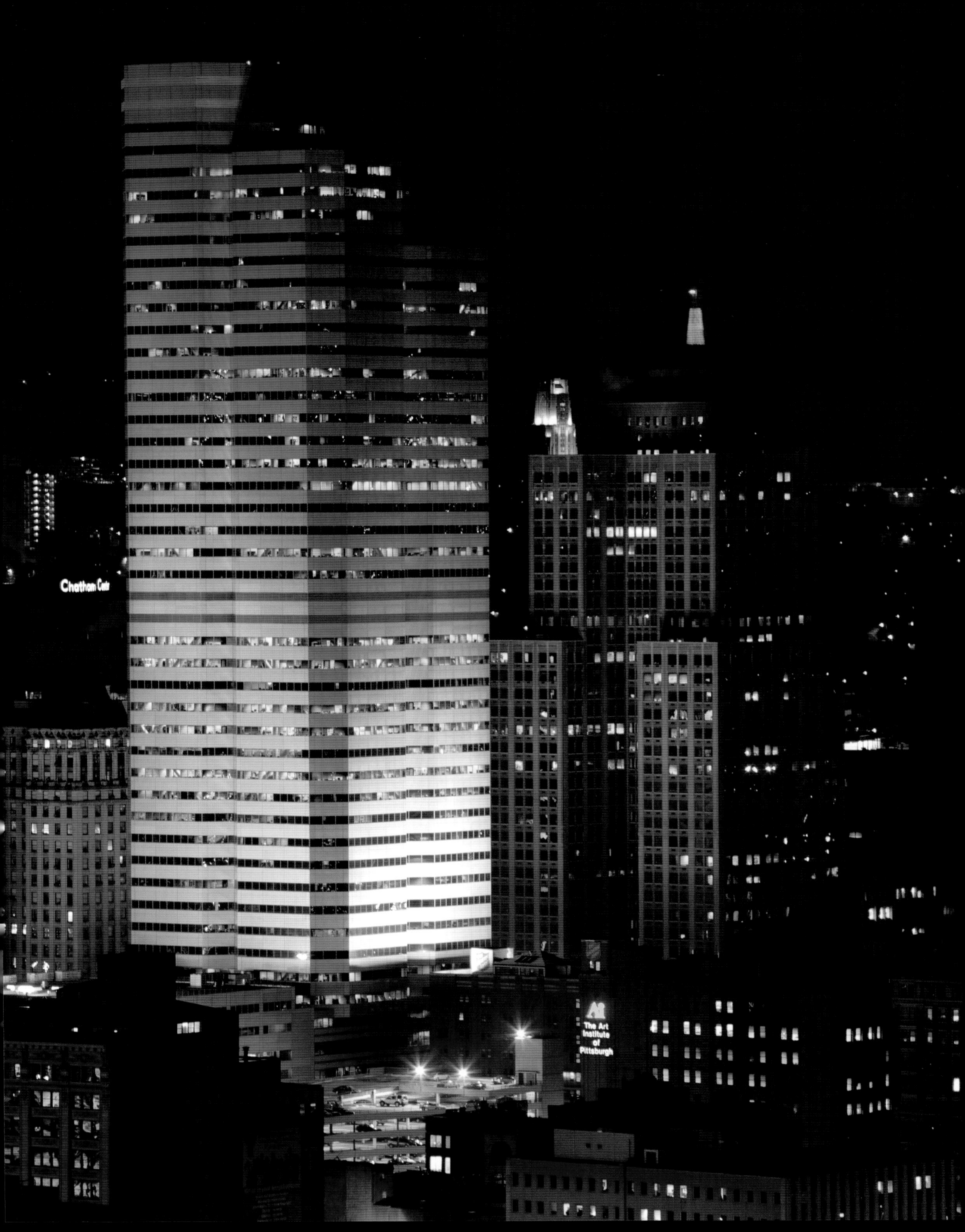
Chatham Center
The Art Institute of Pittsburgh

Fine Dining at Station Square

Grandeur has found a home in the Grand Concourse Restaurant, the former main waiting area for an historic railroad station. World-class cuisine is served in a stately setting of marbled columns, grand pianos, vaulted ceilings, grand staircases, and elegant chandeliers. It is a classic dining experience, from the new outdoor dining space to the distinctive chime of crystal glasses as guests toast an occasion in the main dining room.

Station Square (*above*)

The restored railroad station at Station Square on Pittsburgh's South Side is the centerpiece of an exciting venue of entertainment, dining, and shopping. From the riverfront complex, visitors can ride the cable car to the Mt. Washington scenic overlook, board a boat and tour Pittsburgh's famous rivers, take a romantic horse-and-buggy ride, hop on the Station Square Express train for a tour of the area, or just walk along the riverfront and enjoy the breathtaking views of the city.

Town Square at Southside Works (*pages 36–37*)

Southside Works is a new 34-acre complex of upscale specialty shops, antique stores, bars, ethnic restaurants, offices, high-end apartments, and a cineplex. It is located directly across the Monongahela River from the University of Pittsburgh.

Pennsylvanian Union Station (*opposite*)

Historic Pennsylvanian Union Station enters the 21st century with luxury apartments, offices, retail space, and a fine restaurant. The architecturally-famed rotunda features four destination plaques: Pittsburgh, New York, Philadelphia, and Washington.

River Crossings (*top*)

With Liberty Bridge in the background, a train crosses the Monongahela River on the railroad bridge. The Port Authority of Pittsburgh operates a light rail system called the "T," connecting South Side neighborhoods with the downtown business district.

Grandview Avenue Overlook (*bottom*)

Dusk is the perfect time to come to the Grandview Avenue Overlook on Mount Washington. Here, on Pittsburgh's 400-foot mountain on the South Side, the sky darkens and the city below becomes a sea of twinkling lights.

South Side Slopes at Sunrise *(above)*

Houses appear to be stacked along the steep terrain of Pittsburgh's South Side slopes. Though a walk around these hillside neighborhoods can literally be breathtaking, the fabulous city and river views are well worth the effort.

City of Stairways *(opposite)*

Pittsburgh has some 700 stairways, more than double the number found in San Francisco. More than half of these stair paths have real street signs, yet are simply "paper streets," and have been know to cause some confustion for tourists. In Pittsburgh's early days, the city created the stairways to help people navigate the mountain-goat terrain of many areas. Centuries later, the steps help give the city its unique personality.

Point State Park *(top)*

This picturesque park on the site of historic
Fort Pitt is a popular venue for many of
Pittsburgh's festivals and celebrations. The
three rectangular buildings are recreations
of three of Fort Pitt's original five bastions,
one of which is the Fort Pitt Museum.

Marker at Point State Park *(bottom)*

Twenty-three markers, plaques, and monuments throughout Point State Park celebrate
centuries of Pittsburgh's history as it
evolved from an 18th-century frontier out-
post to one of the most progressive and
dramatically beautiful cities in America.

Point State Park Fountain

A golden sunset and panoramic views create a romantic ambience as the Point State Park fountain careens 150 feet in the air. The massive fountain basin measures 200 feet in diameter. The park also features a riverfront promenade and bike trail.

A Misty Mood

At daybreak, dense fog rolls in from the
west, enveloping the city in an amber
shroud. The mist creates a surreal sunrise,
and the Pittsburgh skyline is a magical
sight, rising above the clouds.

One PPG Place

PPG Center's tallest building creates a majestic crown for the city skyline. The center's six buildings are capped with the 231 distinctive spires and connect historic neo-Gothic architecture with sleeker contemporary buildings in the city.

Sunset at Point State Park

At sunset, walkers enjoy a moment of solitude and scenic views beyond the spray of the fountain at Point State Park. The park was built on the site of historic Fort Pitt, an 18th-century British fort that, due to its position at the headwaters of the Ohio River, served as a strategic stronghold. Developed in 1974, the urban park transformed a neglected area into a scenic, green space that celebrates the origins of Pittsburgh.

Casting on the Allegheny River

A lone fisherman casts out into the shimmering Allegheny River. Pittsburgh has nearly 40 miles of river shorline within its city limits.

McConnell's Mill State Park

Slippery Rock Creek was cut from glacial lakes that drained millions of years ago. The gorge, carved by the rushing waters, is a favorite location for kayakers, hikers, and rock climbers. The park is open most of the year from sunrise to sunset.

Lake Arthur

Surrounded by lush forests and gently rolling hills, Lake Arthur is located one hour north of Pittsburgh in Moraine State Park. With 3,225 acres, this scenic lake is a favorite getaway for boating, swimming, and fishing.

PPG Place Ice Skating Rink

Skaters make the most of a crisp winter day at the PPG Place outdoor skating rink. Its centerpiece is a 44-foot, rose-granite obelisk. During the summer months, the rink becomes a water fountain, creating a pleasant atmosphere for lunch-time crowds.

Agnes Katz Plaza

A 25-foot, spiraling bronze water fountain, created by sculptor Louise Bourgeois, graces the Agnes Katz Plaza. The fountain is illuminated in changing hues in the evening and is surrounded by his equally evocative granite seats that are formed in the shape of human eyes. Located in Pittsburgh's theater district, the plaza was designed by architect Michael Graves; landscape architect, Daniel Urban Kiley; and artist, Louise Bourgeois.

Highland Park Reservoir *(above)*

A runner passes beneath the watchful eye of a bronze eagle in Highland Park. Popular with runners, walkers, and bikers, the park has numerous connecting paths that surround the reservoir.

Winter in Pittsburgh *(opposite)*

A stark wintery scene is highlighted by the bright yellow cast of the Rachel Carson Bridge. Carson grew up just 15 miles from the city. Her pivotal book on the harmful effects of the pesticide DDT led to a ban on its use.

Phipps Conservatory and Botanical Gardens *(left and right)*

The Tropical Forest is the Phipps Conservatory's new multi-million-dollar exhibit that was meticulously designed to be the most environmentally-friendly greenhouse in the world. The exhibit's first section interprets the plants and landscape of Thailand. The topiary-inspired "Mythological Beasts" delight fans of mythological fantasy. The living sculpture (right) is "The Centaur," while others include the "Loch Ness Monster," which is covered with sphagnum-moss.

Magical Gardens *(opposite)*

Thirteen indoor gardens of the acclaimed Phipps Conservatory offer an awe-inspiring tour of international habitats as diverse as a tropical rain forest, a desert, a primordial forest of ferns, a French formal garden, and a Victorian-era greenhouse.

PPG Aquarium *(above, left)*

PPG Aquarium at the Pittsburgh Zoo features a two-story "Open Ocean Tank" where sharks mingle in a diverse ecosystem. Other exhibits include local fish as well as those of the Amazon Rainforest, including piranhas and pacu, known for their human-like teeth.

Jelly Fish Exhibit *(above, right)*

Jellyfish at the PPG Aquarium put on a fascinating show as their translucent, saucer-shaped bodies move through the water with a hypnotic, pulsating action that earns them the nickname, "Sea Lungs."

Gold Breasted Starling *(opposite)*

The National Aviary has over 600 endangered and exotic birds from eco-systems around the world, such as this multi-colored Gold Breasted Starling. The aviary's scheduled bird shows include "Raptor Encounter" and "Penguin Premiere."

Pittsburgh Zoo

The tallest of all herding animals is the reticulated giraffe from the African savanna. Since these giants get moisture from tree-top leaves, it can take as long as one month before they actually get thirsty. In order to eat grass, they must lie down.

Scarlet Ibis (*top*)

This spectacular Scarlet Ibis is fanning and beating his wings at the National Aviary. Its' striking coral and deep pink color attracts the attention of bird watchers.

Bald Eagle (*bottom*)

The National Aviary features a majestic Bald Eagle exhibit. Due to successful conservation efforts in the United States, Bald Eagles were reclassified in 1995 from an endangered species to a threatened species in the lower 48 states.

Mexican War Streets Historical District *(above, and opposite)*

Colorful window boxes decorate a row house in the Mexican War Streets Historic District. North of downtown, this vibrant neighborhood is convenient to many entertainment and cultural venues such as the Children's Museum and Heinz Field.

Streets of this district were named after the generals and battles of the 1846 Mexican War. Built during the 1860s and 70s, the carefully-restored row houses feature Greek revival doorways and stained glass windows.

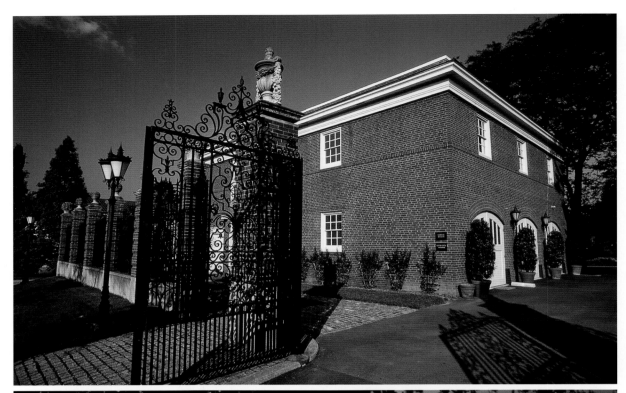

Frick Art and Historical Center *(top)*

The Car and Carriage Museum at the Frick estate in Pittsburgh's East End is part of a five-acre center showcasing the art and philanthropy of industrialist Henry Clay Frick. Frick was the largest producer of coke, which fueled Pittsburgh's steel-making furnaces.

Allegheny Observatory *(bottom)*

Allegheny Observatory is a world-renowned astronomical research institution located eight miles from the University of Pittsburgh. Research is the chief function of the observatory, however, their astronomers also teach classes at the university.

Hazlett Theater *(opposite)*

The Hazlett Theater is attached to the Carnegie Library in Allegheny Center on the Northside of Pittsburgh. It is used for plays, film festivals, and art exhibitions.

Forest Devil (*above*)

Kenneth Snelson's provocative modern art
sculpture is located in the plaza at Mellon
Square. Sixteen stainless-steel tubes are
linked by cables creating a freestanding
structure that symbolizes patterns of physi-
cal forces in space.

Walkway to The Sky (*opposite*)

Internationally-acclaimed for his larger-
than-life sculptures, Jonathan Borofsky
entertains and challenges with *Walkway to
The Sky*, located on the Carnegie-Mellon
University campus. Seven figures climb a
walkway rising 100 feet in the air.

Greenhouse Orchids *(above)*

The Manchester Craftsmen's Guild is a
highly respected public vocational technical
school in Pittsburgh that serves as a launch-
ing pad to higher education. Seventy-five
percent of its graduates go on to four-year
colleges and other career academies.

Magnolias for Pittsburgh

A gray winter day in the Cultural District is interrupted by two magnificent magnolia trees in glorious full bloom. These two bronze, hand-painted sculptures of eternal spring are set amidst five real magnolia trees. According to Chicago sculptor Tony Tasset, the purpose was "to simply create a little magic, a fairy-tale moment in the daily hustle and bustle of downtown Pittsburgh."

Strip District Merchants *(above, left and right)*

As an industrial area in the 1800s and an economic center of Pittsburgh by the 1920s, the "Strip District" continues to reflect an ever-changing city. Today, it is a place of familiar faces, such as Floyd Johnson and his beautiful flower stand and Carol "Dear Heart" Pazucci, who calls everyone "Dear Heart," with many cheeses at the Pennsylvania Macaroni Company. The colorful merchants and their wares are intermingled with "The Strip's" eclectic restaurants, antique shops, and art galleries.

Primanti Brothers Bar & Grill *(opposite)*

Since 1933, Primanti Brothers, at Market Square, has captured the soul of the Pittsburgh sandwich—thick, home-made Italian loaves, sliced just so, filled with cheeses, all kinds of meats, slaw and fries. It's a unique and local classic.

70

Pittsburgh Convention Center *(top)*

Pittsburgh's new convention center has earned the U.S. Green Building Council's "Gold LEED" rating as the first "green" convention center and the world's largest "green" building. It uses natural daylight and ventilation to generate light and heat.

Mellon Arena *(bottom)*

First opened in 1961 as the Civic Arena, The Mellon Arena features a stainless-steel dome that can fully retract in two minutes. The arena is home to National Hockey League's Pittsburgh Penguins and hosts many other entertainment events.

Petersen Event Center

The Petersen Event Center at the University of Pittsburgh is the new 12,500-seat home of the Division I Pitt Panthers basketball team. The center is a flexible venue that accommodates basketball games as well as concerts and commencement ceremonies.

Benedum Center

The Benedum Center is a magnificent reincarnation of a grand building that cost a mere one million dollars to build. The cost of the 1987 restoration was $43 million. There are over 90 crystal chandeliers, torchieres, and sconces in the historic 1927 Stanley Theater and all but one are original. The signature piece of this center is the exquisite, main chandelier which measures 20 feet in height, 12 feet in width, and tips the scales at 4,700 pounds.

Pittsburgh's Cultural District

A Cultural District street flag brightens up a cold winter day. The exuberant district area covers fourteen-blocks in the heart of downtown and offers 44 restaurants, 88 diverse retail shops, five world-class performance venues in which 1,400 performances are held annually, as well as lovely green spaces filled with public art.

Hall of Architecture *(top and bottom)*

The Hall of Architecture at the Carnegie Museum of Art features the country's largest collection of plaster casts of the world's greatest architectural marvels and statuary from ancient Rome and Greece. Opened in 1907, the hall has an extensive collection of over 140 casts. Today, the collection has only two international rivals—London's Victoria and Albert Museum and Paris' National Museum of French Monuments.

Awe-Inspiring *(opposite)*

Natural overhead light highlights the intricate details of the world's masterpieces. The hall itself was modeled after the Mausoleum at Halicarnassus, one of the Seven Wonders of the World.

Heinz Hall for the Performing Arts

A dazzling $10-million renovation of a
grand old movie theater, internationally-
acclaimed Heinz Hall is home to the
Pittsburgh Symphony Orchestra. A corner-
stone of the Cultural District, the hall also
hosts pops concerts and Broadway shows.

Carnegie Museums of Pittsburgh

The unprecedented philanthropy of steel tycoon Andrew Carnegie is evident in the many libraries, museums, and institutions that bear his name in Pittsburgh and other cities across the United States. A massive building on Forbes Avenue houses the Carnegie Institute, the Carnegie Museum of Natural History, and the Carnegie Museum of Art. Carnegie's own fascination with dinosaurs led to the acquisition of "Dippy," the first major dinosaur skeleton ever to be unearthed.

U.S.S. Requiem Submarine

The Carnegie Science Center features the *U.S.S. Requiem*, a World War II submarine. Interactive touch screens in the forward torpedo room, control room, mess deck, berthing compartment, and two engine rooms explain what daily life was like for the eighty sailors on board. Video and audio recordings of *Requiem* veterans add to the experience. The Carnegie Science Center is located next to Heinz Field, the Pittsburgh Steelers' new stadium on the North Shore.

Carnegie Science Center

The marvels of science and discovery come alive at this acclaimed center with stimulating, interactive exhibits. The center features a planetarium and observatory, as well as the OMNIMAX Theater, where viewers experience incredible panoramic video.

Other popular exhibits are SportsWorks®, the world's largest science-of-sport exhibition, and the legendary Miniature Railroad & Village®, with animated scenes of early 20th-century life in western Pennsylvania.

Heinz History Center *(top)*

The largest history museum in the state, the Heinz History Center displays transportation through the centuries, including a pioneers' Conestoga wagon, an antique fire truck, and a vintage, all-stainless-steel automobile by Allegheny Ludlum Corporation.

Points in Time *(bottom)*

A typical 1950s suburban home comes to life with this authentic reconstruction in the Points in Time exhibit. Visitors also experience a 1910 steelworker's home and a vintage 1790 log cabin. This panoramic exhibit covers 250 years of Pennsylvanian history.

Pittsburgh Street Car *(opposite)*

Street cars are powered by overhead electrical current and driven by electric motors. The Light Rail System has replaced the street cars in downtown Pittsburgh, however, the service is still available in the South Hills section.

Photo Antiquities Museum *(top and bottom)*

The Photo Antiquities Museum includes a vast collection of cameras. A tour guide explains the technological advances and breakthroughs that have steadily improved the quality of photographs and have truly made taking pictures a snap.

This display shows a 19th-century daguerreotype of a young boy, an antique mini-camera, and a chemical used to develop the photograph. The museum also has educational programs including "Photo Detective," an observation skills-building session.

Antique Archives

Antique photographs line the shelves of the Photo Antiquities Museum, showcasing the largest collection of 19th-century photographs for public viewing in the country. From the first daguerreotypes in the 1830s to contemporary digital images, a guided tour of photographic history is set amidst the museum's authentic Victorian theme, highlighted with period music. The archives contain over 100,000 negatives and prints, any of which can be reproduced by request. Exhibits change monthly.

Children's Museum *(above, left and right)*

Rain slickers and boots are basic essentials for the interactive Waterplay exhibit at the Children's Museum. When attempting to build a fountain with leaky pipes, children get their first lesson in water pressure. On a drier note, the museum's huge Light Wall and Table is equally fascinating. It's an entire wall filled with giant, illuminated, crayon-colored pegs.

Puppeteering *(opposite)*

A virtual puppet show on a video screen is created with 3-D computer models of the museum's priceless puppet collection. First, puppets are selected, then scenery and music. Joysticks and buttons are then used to make the puppets come alive.

Warhol Museum

With more than 12,000 works of art by Pittsburgh native Andy Warhol, this is the world's most comprehensive museum dedicated to the works of a single artist. The massive collection includes Warhol's paintings, drawings, sculptures, and films.

Mattress Factory Art Museum

At one of the world's most unique museums, contemporary, three-dimensional art surrounds visitors with dramatic appeal. Artists are invited to live at the museum while creating their works. With their living expenses paid, artists are free to follow their vision and build their installation art. "Repetitive Vision II" is a permanent exhibit by internationally-acclaimed Japanese artist, Yayoi Kusama, whose obsession with the repetition of dots became the focus of her most famous works.

89

Hot Air Ballooning

A hot-air balloon pilot inspects his craft as he prepares to take passengers up, up and away at Three Rivers Regatta. The basket is attached to the ground by a long rope which allows passengers to experience the floating sensation without ascending very far.

Lighter than Air

The scientific principle of warm air being lighter than cool air is beautifully demonstrated at Pittsburgh's Three Rivers Regatta. Here, a ballooner gets ready to fire up his burners. The hot air fills the gigantic balloon sending it skyward.

Three Rivers Arts Festival *(top and bottom)*

The aroma of food from around the world mingle in the air, announcing the ethnic diversity of the citizens of Pittsburgh. Many festival goers are descendants of European immigrants who worked the region's coal mines and steel mills. For seventeen days in June, the highly-acclaimed Three Rivers Arts Festival fills the streets with nearly 600,000 people, live performances, and great food. The heart of the festival is the Artists Market where over 350 talented artists display and sell their wares.

Conquering the Wall *(opposite)*

Here, at the Three Rivers Regatta, the smile of a young festival-goer reflects his gaining confidence as he achieves his final goal of conquering the rock-climbing wall.

Kennywood Amusement Park (*top and bottom*)

Located in nearby West Mifflin, the
Kennywood Amusement Park is recognized
as one of the best traditional amusement
parks in America. Dating back to 1883, this
national historic landmark stays thoroughly
modern with exciting new thrill rides.

Schenley Plaza Carousel

A vintage-style carousel is located in Schenley Plaza, the new town square of the Oakland neighborhood. The plaza is part of the $10 million restoration of Schenley Park. In the distance is the University of Pittsburgh's Cathedral of Learning.

Vintage Jaguar Car Show *(above)*

The Vintage Jaguar Car Show is one of many events that attract enthusiastic crowds during Pittsburgh's ten-day Vintage Grand Prix. The challenging race is one of only two in the world where the course runs along regular city streets.

Classic Horsepower *(opposite)*

During the much-anticipated Grand Prix, vintage European sports cars invade Pittsburgh. Many are featured on Schenley Park's grassy slopes, while other favorites vie for position on the challenging twists and turns of the Grand Prix race course.

Moments of Glory (top)

Inside the Heinz History Center is the Western Pennsylvania Sports Museum. The massive exhibit showcases the region's sports legends on the baseball diamond, the football gridiron, in the boxing ring, at NASCAR, or at the Olympic Games.

Motorsports Exhibit (bottom)

Racing enthusiasts who visit the Western Pennsylvania Sports Museum will be thrilled to see the Indy 500 car, owned by Ganassi Racing, that Juan Pablo Montoya raced to victory. It was a great day for Team Target-Ganassi racing.

Pittsburgh's Pennsylvania Motor Speedway

The action is fast and loud at Pittsburgh's Pennsylvania Motor Speedway. Stock car drivers rev their engines along the half-mile dirt track, leaving the competition in the dust. The track features a variety of races from pure stocks to a Young Guns Teen Division.

PNC Park

In 1887, baseball fans witnessed the first game of the new Pittsburgh Pirates franchise. Over a hundred years and five ballparks later, Pittsburgh's affinity with the Pirates is stronger than ever. Fans fill the seats of PNC Park, the Pirates' new downtown facility on the Allegheny River. The ballpark's classic design and natural grass playing field evoke old favorites like Chicago's Wrigley Field and Boston's Fenway Park. Modern amenities abound, and scenic vistas surround this urban park.

Opening Day (top)

Eager Pittsburgh Pirates fans flock to PNC Park for the first game of the season. In the foreground, a bronze sculpture captures a baseball moment full of promise.

Read All About It (bottom)

Opening day makes the headlines of the daily newspaper in this serious baseball town. The Pirates' new ballpark has architectural details reminiscent of Pittsburgh's beloved Forbes Field, the team's previous home for 61 years.

Heinz Field

The familiar Heinz ketchup logo adorns the Pittsburgh Steelers' new home. When the stadium opened, sportscasters affectionately nicknamed it the "Big Ketchup Bottle" and referred to the stadium's bright yellow seats as "Mustard Palace."

Night Game *(top)*

The NFL's Pittsburgh Steelers have commanded their home field for over eight decades with heart-pumping gridiron action. In 2001, the team moved into this new, state-of-the-art, 64,000-seat riverfront stadium.

Stadium by the Riverside *(bottom)*

Commanding a prime riverfront spot, Heinz Field is the Steelers' first "football only" facility. In the past, the team shared Three Rivers Stadium with the Pittsburgh Pirates. University of Pittsburgh football games are also played here.

Pittsburgh Vintage Grand Prix Race

Pittsburgh Vintage Grand Prix Race in Schenley Park is the nation's largest vintage race event and a major fundraiser for disabled citizens of Pittsburgh. Over 200,000 spectators come to the 10-day event. Many come to show off their own antique cars.

Just Ducky *(top)*

Just Ducky Tours provides a totally unique way to see the city of Pittsburgh. A WW II amphibious vehicle treks through the city by land and by river for a fantastic tour experience. Point State Park's beautiful fountain gushes in the distance.

Three Rivers Regatta *(bottom)*

A jet ski stunt performer entertains Fourth of July crowds at Point State Park. The regatta includes two days of entertainment on land and water, including live concerts, powerboat races, dragon boat events, fishing tournaments, and a fireworks finale.

Majestic on the Allegheny (top)

The Gateway Clipper Fleet of sightseeing boats has symbolized Pittsburgh's river renaissance since 1948. The 277-foot *Majestic* is the fleet's new flagship vessel. The boats are authentic reproductions of famed vintage riverboats.

Monongehela River Tug Boat (bottom)

The city of Pittsburgh has transformed its old "Steel Town" image, however, tugboats that guide barges loaded with steel, coal, and slag are still a common sight on the Allegheny, Monongahela, and Ohio rivers.

Firstside Riverfront (opposite)

A tugboat motors along the Monongahela River opposite Ft. Pitt Boulevard/Firstside area. The Port of Pittsburgh is America's second largest inland port. One in six jobs in the region is associated with river traffic.

Motoring In (*above*)

Dwarfed by Gateway Center skyscrapers, a recreational boater enjoys a solitary moment motoring on the Allegheny River as dusk casts its golden light.

USX Tower (*opposite*)

The 68-story USX Tower, formerly the U.S. Steel Tower, is the city's tallest building. It is clad in U.S. Steel's Cor-Ten, a material that resists the corrosive effects of weather. The tower will soon become the corporate headquarters of UPMC Health Insurance.

Reflections (top)

Against a vivid blue sky, the sharp angles of Robert Morris University's façade reflect the neighboring Mellon Financial Center, creating an abstract pattern. The University is a private college with its main campus in the city's Moon Township suburb.

Gateway Center (bottom)

The ambitious development of the seven skyscrapers of Gateway Center played a pivotal role in Pittsburgh's renaissance in the mid-20th century. This prime real estate, located in the "Golden Triangle," is home and headquarters of major corporations.

Mellon Center Two (opposite)

Mellon Center Two is the new address for the former Union Trust Building. Completed in 1917, it was designed by famed Pittsburgh architect Frederick Osterling and pays homage to the 19th-century cathedral previously on the site.

St. Paul's Cathedral

This magnificent cathedral in the Oakland neighborhood is an impressive example of 14th-century Decorated Gothic style and features exterior statues of Saint Paul and other apostles and evangelists. It is the spiritual center of the Diocese of Pittsburgh.

Carnegie Mellon University

The Gothic lines of St. Paul's Cathedral are mirrored in the façade of the neighboring Software Engineering Institute at Carnegie Mellon University. The main campus is located three miles from downtown, adjacent to the University of Pittsburgh.

St. Stanislaus Kostka Church *(above)*

This historic landmark in the city's "Strip District" is one of the city's oldest churches. Built in 1891 in the Old World style of cathedrals, it was once visited by Pope John Paul II as a cardinal. The beauty of the church reminded him of his native Poland.

First Presbyterian Church *(opposite)*

The roots of this historic church reach back to 1787, four years after the Revolutionary War. The original building was made of logs. Over one-hundred years later, this splendid Gothic-style church became the fourth structure of a growing congregation.

Decorative Domes *(pages 116–117)*

The grand "onion" domes of the St. John the Baptist Ukranian Church punctuate a modern skyline and are a tribute to the spiritual life of Ukrainian immigrants who worked the steel mills, coal mines, and factories of 19th-century Pittsburgh.

Campus Life (above, left)

Beyond a kiosk for public notices at the University of Pittsburgh, the neo-Gothic Cathedral of Learning towers above the urban campus and adds its signature style to the city skyline. The University serves a student population of over 30,000.

Cathedral Commons (above, right)

The University of Pittsburgh is one of the country's oldest institutions of higher learning and one of a select group founded in the 18th century. The campus grounds are woven into the heart of the city. Forbes Avenue runs through the campus center.

Cathedral of Learning (opposite)

The vision of former University Chancellor John Bowman during the 1920s, the 42-story Cathedral of Learning is the second tallest education building in the world. Above the three-story Commons Room are classrooms, offices, and on the ground floor, a restaurant.

Soldiers and Sailors Memorial Hall *(top)*

A warm, sunny day brings University of Pittsburgh students to the expansive lawn of the Memorial Hall to sunbathe and study. Built in 1909, the massive building is one of the largest museums in America honoring war veterans.

Sacrifice, Valor, and Patriotism *(bottom)*

Originally conceived by Union Army veterans, this palatial museum has rare exhibits that tell unique stories of American wars fought since the Civil War. The "Hall of Valor" pays tribute to individual veterans from the region.

Pitt's Mascot *(opposite)*

Across from the Cathedral of Learning, the University of Pittsburgh's Panther mascot is poised to pounce. Pitt's athletic teams have made the historic university a sports powerhouse by winning conference titles and national football championships.

Heinz Memorial Chapel

Designed by Philadelphia architect Charles
Z. Klauder, who also designed the Cathedral
of Learning, Heinz Memorial Chapel is a fine
example of the neo-Gothic architecture that
inspired religious and academic buildings
throughout the first half of the 20th century.

Chapel of Distinction *(top and bottom)*

Columns of brilliant, stained-glass windows adorn the towering walls of Indiana limestone, while stone carvings express the Chapel's dedication to spiritual values in education. Polished oak woodworking throughout adds to the chapel's richness.

The non-denominational chapel's detailed stained-glass windows are the work of noted artist and Pennsylvania native Charles J. Connick. He spearheaded the movement to use 13th-century neo-Gothic glass in 20th-century American architecture.

Primary Colors *(opposite)*

Pittsburgh's steel-industry heritage lives on in newer companies like Whemco, that manufactures and repairs steel making equipment. The giant super mills of the early American steel industry eventually gave way to innovative "mini-mills" in the 1980s. Instead of producing steel, updated foundries service steel mills around the world by retrofitting older equipment and casting new mill stands, presses, and other equipment.

Whemco *(top and bottom)*

Machines whirl at Whemco's foundry as pig iron liquefies and new steel making equipment is forged in a red-hot glow. The air in blast furnaces is preheated to temperatures between 1,000 and 1,600 degrees fahrenheit.

Fox Chapel Winter

The rustic and upscale borough of Fox
Chapel at Pittsburgh's northeastern edge is
just six miles from downtown. Located in
Fox Chapel borough are executive homes,
manicured lawns, and natural parks.

Apple Picking in Kilbuck Township

Kilbuck Township is a small division in the Greater Pittsburgh region. With a population of less than 800, its two-and-a-half-square-mile area is just one of Pittsburgh's many suburbs that contribute to the metro area's population of over two million.

Mark Bolster

Born in Elmira, New York, Mark Bolster is one of Pittsburgh's most prolific photographers. His photographs are recognized for his use of graphic composition, and capturing (or creating) moody light and gesture. His work is equally at home in galleries, advertisements, corporate annual reports, private collections, and magazines.

Bolster has photographed professionally since 1976 when he sold his first photograph to designer Tommy Hilfiger. After graduating from the Art Institute of Pittsburgh, Mark assisted over 80 top photographers in New York City, before relocating his now thriving photography business to Pittsburgh in 1985.

Though Mark's assignments have taken him globe trotting to locations around the world, he still enjoys photographing the scenery and buzz of Pittsburgh's neighborhoods, people, corporate leaders, and the stunning beauty of it's rivers, bridges, and architecture.

Bolster was a founding board member and past President of the American Society of Media Photographers Pittsburgh Chapter and has been actively involved in many other photography organizations including, Editorial Photographers and Stock Artists Alliance. He was named Upcoming Photographer by *Art Direction Magazine,* and has been profiled in *Photo District News, Rangefinder, Shutterbug,* and other photography publications.

Mark resides in Pittsburgh with his wife, Elaine and their two sons. He is passionate about auto racing, fishing, and listening to his extensive rhythm and blues and surf music collection.

All photos in this book are available as signed, fine art prints for collectors of fine photography.

To learn more about Bolster and view more of his stunning images please visit www.markbolster.com.